AF711259

LAW FOR A CIRCULAR ECONOMY

LAW FOR A CIRCULAR ECONOMY

Chris Backes

Utrecht Centre for Water,
Oceans and Sustainability Law (UCWOSL)
Inaugural Address, 12 April 2017

Universiteit Utrecht

Utrecht Centre for Water,
Oceans and Sustainability Law

eleven
international publishing

Published, sold and distributed by Eleven International Publishing
P.O. Box 85576
2508 CG The Hague
The Netherlands
Tel.: +31 70 33 070 33
Fax: +31 70 33 070 30
e-mail: sales@elevenpub.nl
www.elevenpub.com

Sold and distributed in USA and Canada
International Specialized Book Services
920 NE 58th Avenue, Suite 300
Portland, OR 97213-3786, USA
Tel: 1-800-944-6190 (toll-free)
Fax: +1-503-280-8832
orders@isbs.com
www.isbs.com

Eleven International Publishing is an imprint of Boom uitgevers Den Haag.

ISBN 978-94-6236-764-7
ISBN 978-94-6274-722-7 (E-book)

Printed in The Netherlands

TABLE OF CONTENTS

1. URGENCY OF CHANGE[1]

I start this lecture with some figures which many of you may already know, at least somehow. I nevertheless want to visualise these facts, because they influence our policy choices and also determine what kind of law we need to realise a circular economy.

The average world citizen has an ecological footprint of about 2.8 global average hectares while there are only 1.7 global hectare[2] of biologically productive land and water per capita on earth.[3]

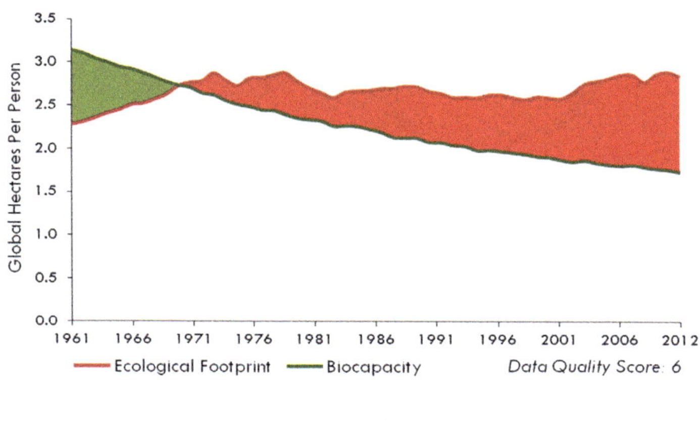

1 Special thanks to John Tieman (ministerie van Infrastructuur en Milieu) and Marga Robesin (Stichting Natuur en Milieu) for their comments on an earlier draft of this address and to Anette Bolton and Jacques Meheut for their advice on language issues.

2 These are globally comparable, standardized hectares with world average productivity.

3 © Global Footprint Network 2016. National Footprint Accounts, 2016 Edition, world graphs.

This means that humanity has already exceeded global biocapacity by more than 60% and now lives unsustainable by depleting stocks of 'natural capital'. The average per country ranges from more than 10 to under 1 hectares per person. By way of example, these are the figures and developments for the US, China, India and the Netherlands:[4 5]

Ecol. Footprint in ha/p	US	Netherlands	India	China
Ecol. Footprint 1961 (appr.)	8,2	3,5	0,7	1,0
Ecol. Footprint 2012	8,2	5,3	1,2	3,4
Change	0	+ 51%	+ 71%	+ 240%

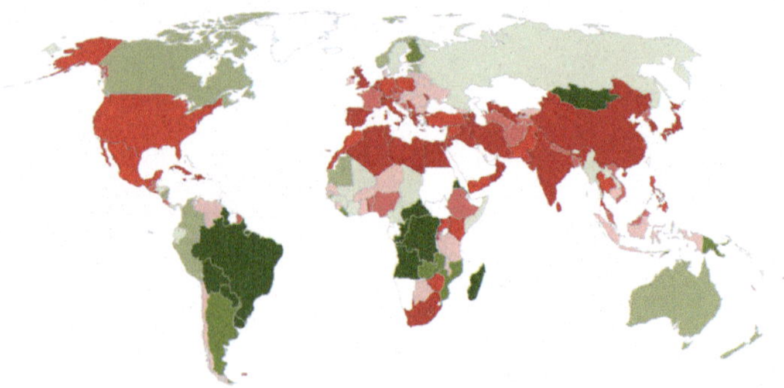

Today humanity uses, on average, the equivalent of 1.6 earths to provide the resources we use and to absorb our waste. In the EU or in the Netherlands, this is much more. If for example

4 National Footprint Accounts 2016 (Data Year 2012); World Development Indicators, The World Bank (2016); U.N. Food and Agriculture Organization, world graphs, Ed. 2016.

5 © Global Footprint Network 2016. National Footprint Accounts, 2016 Edition, world graphs.

everyone would live like we do in the Netherlands we would need approximately 3.1 earths and if we all lived like we do in the US 4.8 earths would be needed.[6] Clearly, this is by no means sustainable.

Therefore, our use of resources must diminish dramatically if we want us, our children and our planet to survive. However, what the world is doing and how it is developing can be illustrated by this chart:[7]

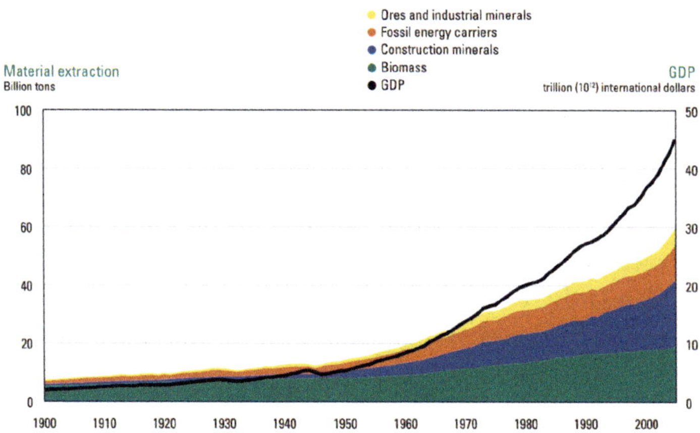

Source: Krausmann *et al.*, 2009

If we will not change our way of life and the emerging countries will adopt our current standards, the global exploitation of resources would multiply by a factor of 3. Therefore, we would

6 I have calculated these figures as follows: average ecological footprint 2012 per country average biocapacity worldwide.

7 M. Fischer-Kowalski et al, Decoupling Natural Resource Use and Environmental Impacts from Economic Growth, UNEP 2011, p. XIV.

not only need three or five earths, but nine or fifteen.[8] Today, I don't want to discuss whether we, in the Netherlands or in Europe, should limit our use of resources to the amount of the resources that our own country produces. I will not discuss whether some countries and some people, like us, should be allowed to consume more resources than others, for example people in India or in African countries. This neither is a sermon, nor a lecture on environmental ethics. Whatever your opinion on this discussion is, and no matter what your choice on 15th March 2017[9] was and whether you work for a NGO or are a CEO of an industrial enterprise, one thing is clear: we have to change our habits and our way of working, consuming and living. A bit of change will not do, we have to reduce our use of primary resources quite dramatically. With regards to the use of fossil energy and CO_2 emissions, there seems to be, at least since the Paris Agreement of November 2015, a common sense of what the targets should be. This was different 15, 20 years ago. With regards to our use of other resources, the discussion seems to be less developed. Although conservation and sparing use of resources has been on the European agenda and some national agendas for at least 15 years,[10] comprehensive long-term targets are not concluded, neither at international, nor at European level and there is no overall strategy. One reason might be that the figures on energy use and CO_2-emissions are relatively easy to calculate and relatively clear. The figures of the actual situation

8 Umweltbundesamt, Ressourenschutzrecht, Position Paper, Berlin Dezember 2013, p. 4.

9 Date of the Dutch elections 2017.

10 See e.g. the Sixth Environmental Action Programme of the EU, Decision No 1600/2002/EC of the European Parliament and of the Council of 22 July 2002; OJ L 242, Article 2 (2) or European Commission, Thematic Strategy on the sustainable use of natural resources, 21 December 2005, COM(2005) 670 final. Or, on national level, e.g. Umweltbundesamt (Hrsg.), Nachhaltige Entwicklung in Deutschland, Berlin 2002, p. 3.

and the prospects of our use and of the stocks of sources other than fossil energy are quite differentiated. Even without being able to rely on concrete targets at the moment, one thing is clear: we cannot go on living and consuming as if we had three, nine or fifteen earths. We only have one earth and therefore should not overexploit its biocapacity. This requires diminishing our consumption of primary resources in Europe by approximately 60%, 80% or 90%.[11]

The Netherlands and some other EU countries seem to belong to the frontrunners in formulating comprehensive strategies and setting targets for the reduction of primary resources. Austria, Finland and Germany, and, since the summer of 2016 also the Netherlands, as well as two regions (Flanders and Scotland) have developed national (or regional) strategies for reducing primary material use and enhancing material efficiency. In 2016, there was not one EU country with comprehensive targets covering the use of all primary materials.[12] In the meantime, the Dutch policy plan on the circular economy seems to have formulated such general targets. In the introductory letter, the government tells us that the 'circular economy' should be 'realised' before 2050 and that in 2030, the Dutch economy should have reduced the use of primary resources by 50%.[13] However, it is not clear, what 'realising the circular economy' means in terms of reduction of the use of primary resources as these are two interrelated,

11 The German Umweltbundesamt estimates that it is necessary to increase the resource productivity by a factor 10; Umweltbundesamt, Ressourenschutzrecht, position paper, Berlin December 2013, p. 4. That would be more less the same as a reduction of the consumption of resources by 90%.

12 European Environment Agency, More from less – material resource efficiency in Europe, EEA Report 10/2016, Kopenhagen 2016, p. 10 f.

13 Rijksbreed programma Circulaire Economie, Kamerstukken II 2015–2016, 32 852, nr. 33, p. 7.

but different things. Furthermore, in the chapter of the plan on 'strategic aims' no figures appear. To enhance the efficiency of political strategies on a sustainable use of resources, concrete mid- and long-term targets seem to be urgently needed on EU and national level. Governments should quickly agree on a common terminology and methodology to measure the use of primary resources and the effectiveness of their reduction policies.

2. CIRCULAR ECONOMY AS A PATHWAY TO SUSTAINABILITY

A pathway to sustainable resource use is the circular economy. A circular economy "is one that is restorative and regenerative by design, and which aims to keep products, components and materials at their highest utility and value at all times, distinguishing between technical and biological cycles".[14] Therefore, the circular economy concept aims at optimising the value of the resources used and to minimise the amount of resources used. However, realisation of the circular economy is not the only way to limit our use of primary materials and by that limiting our ecological footprint. This can for example, to a certain extent, also be done by extending the use of biobased materials. The discussion about the circular economy should, therefore, not substitute the discussion about quantitative targets for the limits of resource consumption.[15] A circular economy is an important pathway to realise the target of the sustainable use of resources, but it is not the same thing. Targets for a sustainable use of primary resources should further be concretised and quantified. In the Netherlands, a basis for this could be the transition agendas,

---

14 Ellen Mac Arthur Foundation, Circular Economy Overview, https://www.ellenmacarthurfoundation.org/circular-economy/overview/concept, lastly reviewed 7 March 2017.

15 The Dutch Social and Economic Council (SER) applies a broader definition of the circular economy than usually used. In the view of the SER, a circular economy is an economy in which materials and products are efficiently and socially responsibly used within the ecological boundaries in order to enable future generations to share prosperity. If such a broad definition is used, circular economy and sustainable use of resources are the same. See for this and other definitions of 'circular economy': Social and Economic Council (SER), Werken aan een circulaire economie: geen tijd te verliezen, The Hague 2016, p. 34.

which are to be developed for five 'priority areas', as has recently been concluded in the Dutch National Agreement on the Circular Economy (Grondstoffenakkoord).[16] According to this agreement, these agendas will define targets for 2021, 2025 and 2030. Similar to decarbonisation being a major guiding principle to realise climate change goals, acting circular must become a major guiding principle to reach these targets and to ensure sustainability of our way of living.

Different from what some people think, a circular economy is not a new way of waste recycling. It is a fundamentally different approach, a radical change of thinking and behaviour. The transition to a circular economy is a systemic change. We have to rethink our ways of producing and consuming. For this transition we will need new technologies, processes, services and business models.[17] There is no choice to opt or not opt for a dramatic reduction of our use of primary resources and for a switch to a circular economy as a pathway to sustainability. We only have one earth and have to change our way of producing and consuming radically to make it sustainable. What we however can choose is to be a frontrunner on this pathway, which probably will offer huge economical possibilities and long-term gains, or to be a follower, which may cost less on investments in the short term.

---

16 National Agreement on the Circular Economy (Grondstoffenakkoord). The agreement was concluded on 24 January 2017 and can be downloaded from https://www.circulaireeconomienederland.nl/grondstoffenakkoord/default.aspx, lastly visited 15 March 2017.

17 European Commission, Closing the Loop – an EU action plan for the Circular Economy, COM (2015), 614 final, p. 18.

3. LEGAL ISSUES AND TRANSDISCIPLINARY CHALLENGES

Enhancing reuse and recycling of waste is only one of the transition tasks. To foster a circular economy, all steps of the product lifecycle have to be addressed: the design, production, use and reuse. And more than that: using a product or using a service instead of owning a product can also contribute to limit the use of primary materials. Fostering the circular economy touches upon and creates a great variety of legal questions. Obviously, new questions in EU and national waste will arise and well known questions in waste law[18] need new answers. One may even ask whether there is still a need for any waste law as there should soon be no or almost no more waste. Should waste law be substituted by legal norms governing materials and products? Even more important than the discussion on waste law may be the questions related to product design and to the use of products. Is the Ecodesign Directive fit for fostering the transition to a circular economy or should it be broadened? Should the Extended Producer Responsibility (EPR) principle be modified? Other questions concern public procurement law or competition law. Recently, my colleague Anna Gerbrandy has published an article about the friction between competition law and circular economy policy and brought forward some ideas to manage these frictions. However, as she has demonstrated, transition to a circular economy urges for a discussion about the basic principles and goals of competition law which is still based on

18 Like what is waste, what is a by-product and when does the qualification as waste end?

neoliberal concepts which do not fit in well with the aims of the circular economy.[19] Also new questions in tax law, consumer law and private law arise. Should the legal rules for accession be changed to promote service contracts? Do we need a review of the minimum warrantee period for certain products?

Working, and hopefully answering some of these legal questions will not bring about the circular economy and will not as such reduce our use of primary materials to a sustainable level. A circular economy demands a system change with parallel actions along the value chain rather than a purely sector or product focused approach. It requires actions in not only the regulatory field but it also requires institutional changes, changes to accounting and financial instruments, cultural changes, technological innovation and knowledge development, and closer cooperation and transparency between all stakeholders. Legal research in this area must be integrated into interdisciplinary teams and projects. Whether and to what extent secondary materials can and will be used in the building of houses is a question which natural scientists, economists, political scientists and lawyers have to discuss and solve together. How the use of insects, that are grown on manure or other kind of waste as food or for the production of food, can be enhanced and how people can be moved to consume this kind of food is amongst others a question of, engineering, behavioural science and law. I look forward to contributing to such interdisciplinary research. Utrecht University has a strong record in sustainability research. The pathway to a circular economy as a topic of

19 A. Gerbrandy, Circulaire economie en de grondslagen van het mededingingsrecht, in: Vereniging voor milieurecht, Met recht naar een circulaire economie, VMR 2017/1, Boom juridisch, Den Haag 2017.

inter- and transdisciplinary research should be strengthened and further developed within this university and beyond.

The fact that this is my forth inaugural address brings about some advantages. However, a disadvantage may be that, until my retirement, only a shorter period of time is left, to elaborate the issues that I deal with in this lecture. Even if I would completely concentrate my future work on the law for a circular economy – which I am not willing to do –, I would not be able to address all legal issues which come along with this topic. Therefore, choices are and will have to be made. For today, only about half an hour is left. I will therefore come to a very short shortlist of legal issues related to the pathways to a circular economy which I will deal with in more detail – related to different topics and, more or less, just by way of example:

- Does the new Dutch Environment and Planning Act (Omgevingswet, Ow) contribute to a transition to a circular economy?
- Do we still need waste law?
- What kind of law do we need to foster circular innovations?

4. THE DUTCH ENVIRONMENT AND PLANNING ACT (OMGEVINGSWET) IS NOT CIRCULAR

I start with a few remarks on the new Dutch Environment and Planning Act (Omgevingswet, Ow). In Dutch environmental and planning law, the introduction of the Environment and Planning Act seems to be so important that it would be unacceptable if the inaugural address of a professor of environmental and planning law did not contain at least some considerations and ideas about this almost historical magnus opus of the Dutch lawmaker. Well, what I have to say about the Dutch Environment and Planning Act and circular economy is that there is not much to say. Or, otherwise put, the new Environment and Planning Act is not circular, it does not substantially support the development of a circular economy. In the explanatory memorandum on the draft act, you will not find the words 'circular economy' or Dutch equivalents. Vice versa, in the recent Dutch policy programme on the circular economy, the Rijksbreed programma circulaire economie, nothing is said about the Environment and Planning Act. What the programme says about law and regulations in general is mainly that existing regulations may hinder innovation and therefore, where they do, should be abandoned. According to the accompanying letter, the recent Crisis- and Recovery Act (Crisis- en herstelwet, Chw) and the forthcoming Environment and Planning Act will foster deregulation and aim to abolish regulations that hinder innovative circular solutions. Additionally, the policy programme 'Ruimte in regels voor Groene Groei'[20] (which perhaps can best be translated as 'prospects within legal rules for green growth') aims at finding solutions in case of constraints caused by the existing legal regime. This is even quantified: until 2016, already 80 restrictions were abandoned and the aim is to remove at least another 80 restrictions until 2020.[21] The role of environmental and planning law, especially the new Environmental and Planning Law Act in fostering a radical transition towards a circular economy seems above all that initiatives and solutions which are developed by the market and by private stakeholders should not be hindered by regulation. At the start of paragraph 4.1 the programme mentions that the circular economy policy should not only aim to abolish legal rules that hinder circular solutions, but that it particularly should develop legal rules that stimulate innovation. However, this is not further mentioned and specified thereafter. Almost all proposed policy actions concern measures to remove barriers. Whether ambitious norms could be concluded to foster innovation is not discussed.[22]

The absence of legal instruments which could foster the transition to a circular economy in the Environment and Planning Act may to a great extent be explained by the fact that the law on materials and products is not yet integrated into the new Environment and Planning Act. Although there is room for this in the table of content (chapters 6, 7 and 8), the question is whether product regulation ever will find its legal basis in in the Environment and Planning Act. It seems that the further development of

20 Often referred to as R2G2; http://www.ruimteinregels.nl/, lastly reviewed 15 March 2017.

21 Rijksbreed programma Circulaire Economie, Kamerstukken II 2015–2016, 32 852, nr. 33, bijlage, p. 25.

22 Rijksbreed programma Circulaire Economie, Kamerstukken II 2015–2016, 32 852, nr. 33, bijlage, p. 25 ff.

the regulation of materials and products and the Environment and Planning Act are two almost totally separated tracks. This however is not only a question of law making technique and the right order within the Dutch environmental and planning law. It is also a question of focus, or, perhaps more correctly: the lack of focus. Whether the Environment and Planning Act optimally supports the fundamental transitions to sustainability, like decarbonisation and circularity, has not been the focus of the lawmaker. The lawmaker mainly aimed at a more flexible, faster decision-making and more decentralisation.

5. REGULATING PRODUCTS INSTEAD OF WASTE LAW?

I will not deeply discuss waste law issues today. Waste law was the topic of my first inaugural lecture, back in 1996. However, there is one principal question which should be dealt with: do we still need waste law at all or can and should it be substituted completely or as far as possible by material- and product regulation? The simple idea is: in a 'zero-waste society',[23] waste no longer exists, but only secondary materials. Therefore, waste law does not seem to be necessary any longer. The environmental risks of materials can be managed by applying material or product regulations. There are four reasons which are not favourable for the applicability of waste law:[24]

- Waste has a negative image. Companies that recover or recycle secondary materials do not want to be associated with waste processors. This may hinder circular use of materials.
- Handling waste means extra administrative burdens. Companies which deal with waste do need a special permit (or an extra review and extra provisions in their integrated permit). This is all the more true for transboundary shipment of waste. This also means a financial burden. And, it hinders innovation.[25] If a new idea to recycle something is qualified as a waste recovery operation, a company which does

23 Commissie Duurzaamheidsvraagstukken Biomassa (Commissie Corbey), Advies Afval: Duurzaam gebruik en beheer van biomassastromen, 2017, p. 3.

24 See e.g. Commissie Duurzaamheidsvraagstukken Biomassa (Commissie Corbey), Advies Afval: Duurzaam gebruik en beheer van biomassastromen, 2017, p. 9.

25 See also Rijksbreed programma Circulaire Economie, p. 26.

not have a licence to treat this sort of waste is not allowed to apply the new circular solution. In such a case, the company has to apply for a new licence first, which will take months or more likely even years.

- Waste law is an 'unsafe area'. If one thing is clear: the interpretation of 'waste' and other crucial waste law terms is not clear, not even after a huge amount of case law of the European Court of Justice on this issue.[26] This legal uncertainty hinders innovative circular solutions.

Therefore, there may be some good reasons to limit the scope of waste law.[27] Some even plea that in the future, waste law should only be used where it is "undisputed" ("onomstreden") that waste law is needed and environmental risks cannot be controlled otherwise.[28] This leads us to the question why we have and need waste law and what its function is. The answer is twofold: Waste law wants to prevent environmental risks due to the fact that materials which are waste may be a burden for the holder. If an issue cannot be used for its original purpose one may want or even need to get rid of it. Uncontrolled disposal or even dumping of waste causes very serious environmental risks. With regards to this function, waste law is not needed if

26 See in more detail: J.R.C. Tieman, Naar een nuttige toepassing van het begrip afvalstof, Kluwer, Deventer 2003 and recently J.R.C. Tieman, Afval of grondstof in een circulaire economie – op zoek naar meer rechtszekerheid, in: Vereniging voor Milieurecht, Met recht naar een circulaire economie, VMR 2017/1, Boom juridisch, Den Haag 2017.

27 Rijksbreed programma Circulaire Economie, p. 25; Tieman 2017, ; R.G.J. Laan, Circulaire economie gebaat bij non-circulaire rechtspraak, in: Vereniging voor Milieurecht, Met recht naar een circulaire economie, VMR 2017/1, Boom juridisch, Den Haag 2017.

28 Laan 2017; See also F. van Eijk/Acceleratio, Barriers & Drivers towards a Circular Economy, Naarden, March 2015, p. 11; to be downloaded at http://www.circulairondernemen.nl/uploads/e00e8643951aef8adde612123e824493.pdf, lastly reviewed 3 March 2017.

the materials can be reused or recycled and, as a consequence, the materials still have an economic value for the holder. From this perspective, waste law is redundant as soon as it is assured:

- that goods or materials are reused or recycled,
- that this reuse or recycling is in accordance with all legal requirements
- and that it still has a positive value for the holder.

However, waste law has (at least) a second function.[29] By regulating waste, governments try to ensure a high level and high quality of reuse, recovery or recycle operations.[30] Long before the term circular economy was introduced in the EU and the Netherlands, policy and law tried to ensure that the value of waste operations was as high as possible. To use only the caloric value of materials by burning them is environmentally much less precious than re-using the materials itself for a different purpose. That is why there are waste hierarchies and ladders of waste operations that have been in place since the nineteen-seventies.[31] The waste hierarchy[32] aims to encourage the options that deliver the best overall environmental outcome. The legally binding targets in EU waste legislation have been a key motor to improve waste management practices, stimulate innovation in recycling and create incentives to change consumer behaviour.[33] However, in practice this honourable and demanding principle is not always applied and the success of the policy partly depends on

29 Also Tieman 2017, par. 3.1 points this out.
30 Directive 2008/98/EG, Article 11 and consideration 6 and 7.
31 See Ontwerp derde Landelijk Afvalbeheerplan 2017-2029, p. 28.
32 See Article 4 Waste Framework Directive.
33 European Commission, Proposal for amending directive 2008/98/EC, SWD (2015) 259 final, p. 2.

markets.[34] If the regulations on materials and products are not suitable to address these issues and if they are not assured otherwise, limiting the scope of waste law does not seem advisable. Considerations to limit the scope of waste law should not only focus on the need to manage environmental risks of materials and products[35], but should take both functions of waste law into account. Waste law should not be abolished if one of the following conditions applies:

- It is not sure that the goods and materials at stake will be kept within the economy (circular use).
- The goods and materials do not anymore have a positive value for the holder.
- There is no legal regime that enables the government to assure a high level of the (re)use of the materials or goods and the prevention of risks to health and environment.

Substitution of waste law should only be considered if the loss of steering capacity is outweighed by the benefits of encouraging innovation and market solutions for a high level reuse. To some extent, this can be characterised as a catch 22-situation: waste law is there to stimulate and guarantee a high level of circular use of materials. However, because of the applicability of waste law the markets do not develop the highest possible circular use of materials. On the way to a circular economy, waste law will more and more be replaced by 'resources law'. This 'resources law' will have to ensure that the risks for humans and the envi-

34 See e.g. G.C. Bergsma, J. Vroonhof, M.J. Blom, I.Y.R. Odegard, Evaluatie Landelijk Afvalbeheersplan (LAP) 1n en 2, CE Delft, Delft 2014, p. 6 ff.

35 In practice, the scope of the discussion is limited to this aspect only; see e.g. Commissie Duurzaamheidsvraagstukken Biomassa (Commissie Corbey), Advies Afval: Duurzaam gebruik en beheer van biomassastromen, 2017, p. 10 ff or Laan 2017.

ronment of using secondary materials are controlled and that the highest possible level of reuse is ensured.

Let's take a quick look at whether and how these criteria are dealt with in the actual European discussion on the scope of waste law. I will concentrate on the question whether the definition of 'waste' should be further clarified or altered and whether the exception for so-called by-products in Article 5 of the waste framework directive is adequate. The relation between waste-law and product- and material-regulations is complicated and challenging. This topic is dealt with in several contributions to a publication of the Dutch Environmental Law Society which will soon be published.[36] In the Commission's proposal for an amendment to the waste framework directive, the definition of 'waste' is not changed. An attempt of the Dutch government to further specify the current definition of "discard" within the definition of 'waste' in Article 3 of the Waste Framework Directive was not taken on. The Dutch wanted to expressly refer to three elements: any materials or goods which *for sure are (re)used* should not be treated as waste if this use is *lawful* and contributes to an *efficient use of primary materials*.[37] At first sight, this proposal seems to refer to all the elements mentioned above. The ambition of a high level of circular use of materials is addressed in the need of an *efficient* use of primary materials. The problem however seems to be that the question whether materials are *efficiently* used, hence whether a high level of circular use

36 Vereniging voor Milieurecht, Met recht naar een circulaire economie, VMR 2017-1, Boom juridisch, Den Haag 2017, especially the contributions of Donner, Tieman and Keessen.

37 The only publically traceable source of this proposals seems to be footnote 51 on p. 42 of Commissie Duurzaamheidsvraagstukken Biomassa (Commissie Corbey), Advies Afval: Duurzaam gebruik en beheer van biomassastromen, 2017.

is ensured, is an element of the definition of waste itself. That may be even more complicated to assess than the current criteria whether the holder discards or intends or is required to discard something. Therefore the decision of the Commission not to change the definition of 'waste' itself, but to further clarify, enlarge and strengthen the definitions of the exceptions of the qualification as 'waste' in Article 5 and 6 of directive 2008/98/EC seems to be wise. However, there seems to be no good reason for limiting the exception of Article 5 of directive 2008/98/EC to by-products. It should not be decisive whether 'the substance or object is produced as an integral part of a production process'. The rationale of Article 5 directive 2008/98/EC does applies to all kind of materials and goods. Furthermore, one could think of opening the possibility for the Commission to exclude, on a case by case basis, certain substances or goods from the waste regime if (a) further use is certain, (b) lawful and (c) contributes to the high(est) level of efficient use of primary materials. The end-of-waste-criteria of Article 6 directive 2008/98/EC seem to be insufficient for this aim as they exclude the waste regime only after a certain treatment of a good which in the first instance has been qualified as waste and has been subject to waste regulations. Such a possibility to exclude the application of waste law would make it possible to foster and enhance circular solutions which may now be hindered by the applicability of waste law if it is proven that the continued (re)use will not contravene waste hierarchy strategies and other environmental and resource efficiency requirements and goals.

The power of the EU Commission to decide on the applicability of such an exception would come along with some advantages, but also with some disadvantages. An advantage would be that the rules for European Regulation on the Shipments of Waste (regulation 1013/2006/EC) is also excluded. Therefore, the goods or materials do not have to deal with the administrative and financial burdens of this regulation. Furthermore, excluding a certain reuse of certain materials or goods from the qualification of 'waste', fosters this way of usage all over Europe and may encourage competition within the EU. If a new circular solutions is invented in one member state and excluded from waste law, (companies in) other member states may also want to make use of this exception. However, there is also a disadvantage. A decision on the exception of the waste regime on EU level takes time. Companies with ideas for innovative solutions may not have the time or money to await the results of such a process. As it is not an option to empower national authorities to make exceptions on the legal qualification of waste, a solution to this problem is not easy. A part of a solution is already available now. National authorities can of course exclude the application of certain requirements of national waste law until the European Commission has decided.[38] However, transboundary shipments of such materials still falls under the EU regulation on transboundary shipments of waste. Therefore, the administrative and financial burdens of this regulation remain to apply.

38 See e.g. the Dutch article 22.1, sub 10, Environmental Code (Wet milieubeheer) which excludes reuse of certain substances as animal feed from the application of the Dutch waste law requirements. See also some of the exceptions in Article 10.1a Environmental Code.

6. HOW TO FOSTER INNOVATIONS?[39]

If we want to become a by and large circular economy within a few decades, innovative products and solutions have to be introduced. [40] For a legal scholar, an important question then is, what kind of law supports innovations and what kind of legal requirements do the opposite, hence are barriers for innovations? In scholarly discussions in planning and environmental law within the Netherland and also within Europe, this question is not discussed intensively. As far as the Netherlands are concerned, Heldeweg dedicated a part of his inaugural address to this question in 2009.[41] Recently Verschuuren en Bink published a report on this topic, composed on behalf of the Ministry of Infrastructure and the Environment.[42] These authors mainly rely on publications of US scholars about environmental law fostering innovations. After a broad review of (mainly) US literature, Verschuuren and Bink conclude that, despite many

39 Some of the following, namely paragraphs 6., 6.1, 6.2 and 6.4, corresponds to a substantial degree with a publication in Dutch, Faciliteert het omgevingsrecht innovaties op weg naar een circulaire economie? In: Vereniging voor milieurecht, Met recht naar een circulaire economie, VMR 2017/1, Boom juridisch, Den Haag 2017, which will be published in the autumn of 2017.

40 About the importance of (different kinds of) innovations for the circular economy: Social and Economic Council (SER), Werken aan een circulaire economie: geen tijd te verliezen, The Hague 2016, p. 73 ff.

41 Zie bijvoorbeeld M.A. Heldeweg, Smart rules and regimes, publiekrechtelijk(e) ontwerpen voor privatisering en technologische innovatie (oratie Universiteit Twente), 24 september 2009, https://www.utwente.nl/academischeplechtigheden/oraties/archief/2007-2014/oratieboekje_heldeweg.pdf, p. 155 e.v.

42 J. Verschuuren, K. Bink, Naar slimme milieuregelgeving die innovatie stimuleert, Tilburg University 2015, https://pure.uvt.nl/portal/files/6577524/Naar_slimme_milieuregelgeving_die_innovatie_stimuleert_eindrapport260215_anon.pdf; zie ook J. Verschuuren, Innovatie en milieuregelgeving, M en R 2015, p. 113 e.v.

controversies, three findings seem to be robust and approved by almost all scholars, writing on this topic:

- "Far reaching (strong) environmental goals which are fixed for a long period of time are a crucial prerequisite for realising radical innovations;[43]
- incremental innovations are facilitated by environmental goals which are sharpened at times;
- if the legislator chooses to sharpen the environmental goals stepwise, radical innovations are almost barred."[44]

According to Porter and Van de Linde[45] environmental regulation which wants to foster innovations should furthermore:

- leave the industry the maximum freedom for finding innovative solutions; the lawmaker must not prescribe how the ambitious goals should be realised;
- stimulate continuous improvement, but should not be aimed at realising a certain technology;
- provide as much predictability and security as possible.[46]

The legal framework is only one element needed to foster innovations. Other factors are for example a good knowledge of infrastructure, financing possibilities, promising business cases etc. Even if the legal framework is adequate, innovations will not

---

43 Different from incrimental innovations, radical innovations are based on, respectively mean (technological) breakthroughs, a completely new product, service or process, which functions independent from existing products, services or processes.

44 J. Verschuuren, K. Bink, Naar slimme milieuregelgeving die innovatie stimuleert, Tilburg University 2015, p. 5 e.v. own translation (Ch.B.)

45 M.E. Porter, C. van der Linde, Toward a New Conception of the Environment-Competitiveness Relationship, Journal of Economic Perspectives Vol. 9, 1995, p. 97 ff.

46 J. Verschuuren, K. Bink, Naar slimme milieuregelgeving die innovatie stimuleert, Tilburg University 2015, p. 7.

appear if all other factors are not favourable. I will use the findings mentioned above as a point of departure and benchmark for the analyses of European and Dutch circular economy policy and law. Is the existing and proposed European[47] and Dutch[48] law suitable to promote innovations for a circular economy? I will research this question only with regards to a few examples mentioned in the recent European and Dutch circular economy programmes.

6.1 LEGAL REGIME OF PRODUCTION PROCESSES

According to the action programme, the European Commission tries to enhance resource efficiency in production processes mainly by including this aspect in the BREF documents which, on the basis of the IE-Directive have to be taken into account in licensing installations falling under the scope of this directive.[49] The BREF documents reflect the techniques that are applied in practice within Europe and have been proven to be economically and technically feasible.[50] Trying to support circular production by regulating circular economy issues via the BREF documents will not foster innovations. It concentrates on the status quo and is above all an instrument to disseminate proven techniques throughout Europe, hence to ensure the level playing field within the respective sector of industry. An example to illustrate this is the most recent (January 2017) published draft BREF-document, which concerns the Food, Drink and Milk

---

47 European Commission, Closing the Loop – an EU action plan for the Circular Economy, COM(2015), 614 final

48 Rijksbreed programma Circulaire Economie, Kamerstukken II 2015–2016, 32 852, nr. 33, bijlage.

49 Directive 2010/75/EU, IE-Directive.

50 See the definition of BREF in Article 3 Directive 2010/75/EU (IE-Directive).

Industry.[51] Referring to the circular economy strategy it mentions: "The potential role of treated waste water as an alternative source of water supply is now well acknowledged and embedded within European and national strategies." What follows is a description of well-equipped and broadly used techniques to reuse treated waste water as "examples of good environmental practices".[52] All the aforementioned issues must be taken into consideration when evaluating the water consumption and considering water reuse and recycling in a specific installation.[53] BREF-documents therefore sum up techniques which are already commonly used and provide orientation for those installations which do not yet use such techniques. Their function is to limit differences between the emission levels of industry throughout Europe and to create equal competition between all enterprises in a certain sector of production, as the preamble of the directive explicitly mentions.[54] I don't plea against integrating circularity aspects into the BREF-documents, as this contributes to a faster dissemination of solutions which already have proven to be feasible on a large scale throughout Europe, but this does not encourage innovations.

However, there is an indirect way to make use of production regulation for fostering circular innovations. The IE-Directive

---

51 This BREF document can be found at http://eippcb.jrc.ec.europa.eu/reference/BREF/FDM/FDM_31-01-2017-D1_b_w.pdf (lastly reviewed 27 February 2017).

52 Another similar example of dealing with circular economy issues in recent BREF-documents: par. 4.25.4.5 (p. 615) of the BREF-document Refining of Mineral Oil and Gas of 2015; eippcb.jrc.ec.europa.eu/reference/ref.html (lastly reviewed 27 February 2017).

53 Best Available Techniques (BAT) Reference Document in the Food, Drink and Milk Industries, First Draft, http://eippcb.jrc.ec.europa.eu/reference/BREF/FDM/FDM_31-01-2017-D1_b_w.pdf (lastly reviewed 27 February 2017), p. 67 en 68.

54 See preamble 3 and 13 of the IE-Directive.

only sets minimum standards for installations. Member States may prescribe stronger requirements. Article 14 (4) IE-Directive stresses that member states may "set stricter permit requirements than those achievable by the use of best available techniques". In Dutch law this is reflected by Article 2.14 (1) (c) (1) Environmental and Planning Law General Provisions Act (Wet algemene bepalingen omgevingsrecht, Wabo), which generally requires that permit conditions should "at least" reflect the best available techniques. Therefore, national (or regional) governments can for sure go beyond BAT and beyond the BREF documents. They could prescribe ambitious requirements in general rules setting standards for IE-permits for certain types of installations. For example, they could prescribe much higher percentages than usually applied at the moment for the use of secondary materials in permits for clinker production or cement plants. In the end and indirectly, the new techniques would then find their way into the BREF documents sometime in the future to be disseminated throughout Europe. Furthermore according to Article 27 (1) IE-Directive, "member states shall, where appropriate, encourage the development and application of emerging techniques...". The Commission can, according to Article 27 (2) IE-Directive, "establish guidance to assist member states in encouraging the development and application of emerging techniques". As far as I know, this instrument has never been used until now. One could consider applying it with the aim of promoting innovations for circular production. However, it does not meet the criteria, identified above very well. Regulation should concentrate on environmental goals and norms for circularity, not on techniques.

We therefore can conclude that the regulation of production on EU level, which is mainly steered by the IE-Directive, is not designed to foster innovations for a circular economy. However, regulation of production can be used for that purpose, but only if some national governments take the lead and prescribe circular economy norms in general rules on permit conditions which go much beyond BAT and beyond what is required by European law. Usually, the default option in environmental law (and policy) often is to concentrate on transposing and applying EU law requirements and to prevent any goldplating. To push innovations, the default cannot be used and the order should be upturned. National governments and national environmental law should take the lead and EU law will follow. It is a pity that the Dutch policy plan on the circular economy, the Rijksbreed Programma Circulaire Economie does not discuss this option at all. This is a missed opportunity.

If in the Netherlands the regulation of production, hence the permitting of installations, is used to promote innovation for a circular economy, a few aspects have to be taken into account. If ambitious circularity criteria for certain types of installations are set, they have to be drafted as criteria which can justify the refusal of a request for a permit. Competent authorities are not allowed to add such conditions on their own to permits for installations, if techniques which comply with these criteria are not entailed in the permit request. When setting the permit conditions, the authorities may not substantially deviate from what is requested. The courts otherwise rule that the authority tries to permit 'a different kind of installation' than the one which was requested.[55] The competent authorities therefore have to be empowered to refuse an application if this application does not meet the ambitious circularity criteria defined for the respec-

55 For example ABRvS 12 September 2000, M en R 2001, 21.

tive kind of installations. Furthermore, is has to be taken into account that permits for industrial installations may only regulate the production process and may not contain requirements for the products.[56] According to the enumeration of aspects that may be subject to the rules of the Dutch central government on industrial activities in Article 4.22 of the Environment and Planning Act, all this will not change when the Environment and Planning Act comes into effect.

6.2 REGULATION OF MATERIALS AND PRODUCTS: ECODESIGN DIRECTIVE 2009/125/EC

EU law comprises a whole range of measures regulating products. Some concern specific products,[57] others certain, limited aspects of product regulation like labelling. The most important measures to be mentioned here may be:[58]

- Ecodesign Directive, Directive 2009/125/EC
- Energy Labelling Directive, Directive 2010/30/EU
- REACH Regulation, Regulation 1907/2006/EC, REACH
- Construction Products Regulation, Regulation 305/2011/EU
- Waste Electrical and Electronical Equipment (WEEE)-Directive, Directive 2012/19/EU

As the Ecodesign Directive may have the highest potential for promoting circular economy issues, I will concentrate on this measure. The full name of the directive better indicates its purpose: "Directive 2009/125/EC ... establishing a framework for the setting of ecodesign requirements for energy related products".

56 Zie ook hiervoor ABRvS 12 September 2000, M en R 2001, 21.

57 Like directive 2000/53/EC on end-of-life vehicles.

58 See also the overview at J. Sanden Aktuelle Analyse des europäischen Ressourcenschutzrechts, UBA Texte 84/2015, Berlin 2015, p. 29 ff.

Hence, actually, the scope of the directive is limited. The aim is to prevent barriers to trade and unfair competition caused by disparities between the laws or administrative measures adopted by the Member States in relation to the ecodesign of energy-related products. Furthermore, the directive wants to encourage improvement of the overall environmental impact of energy-related products "in the interest of sustainable development". According to Article 1 (2), "it contributes to sustainable development by increasing energy efficiency and the level of protection of the environment". The directive covers potentially all products that have an impact on energy consumption during their use (Article 2, sub 1). Products falling under the scope of the directive may be placed on the market only if they bear the CE marking sign. This sign may only be affixed to a product if it complies with the requirements prescribed in the directive and its annexes. If a product has a CE-mark, member states are, according to Article 6, no longer allowed to prohibit, restrict or impede the placing on the market or the putting into service on grounds of ecodesign requirements relating to those covered by the directive.

As Annex I makes clear, the criteria that may be taken into account when setting the requirements to gain the CE-mark may relate to all phases of the lifecycle of the product:

(a) raw materials selection and use;
(b) manufacturing;
(c) packaging, transport, and distribution;
(d) installation and maintenance;
(e) use;
(f) end-of-life, meaning the state of a product having reached the end of its first use until its final disposal.

For each phase, the following environmental aspects must be assessed where relevant:

(a) predicted consumption of materials, of energy and of other resources such as fresh water;
(b) anticipated emissions to air, water or soil;
(c) anticipated pollution through physical effects such as noise, vibration, radiation, electromagnetic fields;
(d) expected generation of waste material;
(e) possibilities for reuse, recycling and recovery of materials and/or of energy, taking into account Directive 2002/96/EC.

Evaluating the potential for improving the environmental aspects of the goods, the following parameters must be used, "as appropriate, and supplemented by others, where necessary,":

(a) weight and volume of the product;
(b) use of materials issued from recycling activities;
(c) consumption of energy, water and other resources throughout the lifecycle;
(d) use of substances classified as hazardous to health and/or the environment;
(e) quantity and nature of consumables needed for proper use and maintenance;
(f) ease for reuse and recycling as expressed through: number of materials and components used, use of standard components, time necessary for disassembly, complexity of tools necessary for disassembly, use of component and material coding standards for the identification of components and materials suitable for reuse and recycling (including marking of plastic parts in accordance with ISO standards), use of easily recyclable materials, easy access to valuable and other recyclable components and materials, easy access

to components and materials containing hazardous substances;

(g) incorporation of used components;

(h) avoidance of technical solutions detrimental to reuse and recycling of components and whole appliances;

(i) extension of lifetime as expressed through: minimum guaranteed lifetime, minimum time for availability of spare parts, modularity, upgradeability, reparability;

(j) amounts of waste generated and amounts of hazardous waste generated;

(k) emissions to air;

(l) emissions to water;

(m) emissions to soil.

This, even not comprehensive, quotation of parts of Annex I of the directive demonstrates two things. First, the directive potentially addresses all aspects relevant with regards to a more circular design of products. Hence, the directive has a huge potential to serve as a legal basis for setting ambitious requirements encouraging innovations.[59] Second, the recital demonstrates that regulating products on the basis of this directive may become very complex and detailed. The regulator has to make sure that, if a holistic view on the environmental aspects of products is aimed at, the rules do not prescribe certain techniques or processes, but only define results and outcomes to be reached and

59 I will not deal here with the insufficient control and enforcement of EU product law, which, for example is addressed in: European Parliament, Committee of Inquiry into Emission Measurements in the Automotive Sector, Final report, http://www.europarl.europa.eu/sides/getDoc.do?type=REPORT&mode=XML&reference=A8-2017-0049&language=EN (lastly reviewed 15 March 2017); see also H.E. Woldendorp, Het verkeerslicht springt op oranje!, M en R 2017, 95 e.v. Obviously, deficiencies in control and enforcement of product law diminish its effectiveness.

thus leaving the industry maximum freedom in how to realise these outcomes. Otherwise, the sum of the requirements set on the basis of Annex I will not encourage, but hinder innovation.

Currently however, the scope of the requirements based on the Ecodesign Directive is much more limited to almost only energy efficiency targets. If the lawmaker wants to use the Ecodesign Directive to promote circular products and especially to encourage innovation in this area, he may choose between two ways forward. The lawmaker could concentrate on certain aspects of certain (groups of) products where regulation is urgent and promises to be very efficient. For example, this could concern the amount of secondary materials used or the ease to be disassembled and reused.[60] However, such sporadic regulation of bits and pieces of circularity comes along with some disadvantages. It is less stable and predictable and there is a higher danger of unintended side effects. Therefore, alternatively setting standards for certain (groups of) products on the basis of holistic lifecycle analyses seems to be preferable. I will come back to the need and capability to set and determine such holistic criteria when discussing circularity in the construction and building sector.

According to Article 17 Ecodesign Directive, voluntary agreements or other self-regulation measures should be assessed as alternatives for regulation. Self-regulation has certain advantages compared with public law regulation. From the point of view of fostering innovations, self-regulation however only

60 Th. Schomerus, L. Spengler, Integration der Ressourceneffizienz in die Ökodesign Richtlinie – Regelungsrahmen und Regelungsmöglichkeiten – Arbeitspapier, http://www.eup-network.de/fileadmin/user_upload/Produktgruppen/V_526-3_Arbeitspapier_-_Regelungsrahmen_und_Moeglichkeiten__AP2_.pdf(lastlyreviewed 10 February 2017) doubt whether the directive allows this kind of approach, focussed on one or only some aspects of circularity.

is preferable if the requirements applied in the self-regulation schemes are sufficiently ambitious, verifiable and, if self-regulation proves to be ineffective, enforceable. Annex VIII of the directive addresses these issues. Importantly, criterion 4 of Annex VIII is relevant here. Next to these criteria, the requirements of voluntary schemes should be ambitious enough to be a motor for innovations. Therefore, it may, in general, not be possible to comply with these requirements by continuing business as usual or with limited adjustment only.

An important issue is that the scope of the Ecodesign Directive is currently limited to energy-related products. The directive is currently applied to products which consume much energy during their use, like televisions,[61] consumer refrigerators and freezers,[62] washing machines[63] and dishwashers.[64] The purpose of these regulations is almost completely limited to lowering the use of energy. None of the regulations issued on the basis of the Ecodesign Directive aim for example at encouraging the reuse of recycled or other secondary materials or on the ease of the recovery or reuse of parts of the products after their intended use has ended. The limitation to 'energy-related products' limits the scope of the directive to some extent. According to Article 2 sub 1 Ecodesign Directive, 'energy related product' is defined as a "good that has an impact on energy consumption during use". Therefore, not only products or goods which consume energy during their use fall under the directive, but also products which have any effect on the use of energy, for example isola-

61 Regulation 642/2009/EC which currently is being revised.

62 Regulation 643/2009/EC.

63 Regulation 1015/2010/EC.

64 Regulation 1016/2010/EC. An overview of all existing and proposed implementation instruments can be found at: http://www.eup-network.de/de/produktgruppen/entwuerfe-verordnungen.

tion material, wirings and windows. However, there are limits. Not all construction materials fall under the scope of the directive. From the viewpoint of supporting the transformation to a circular economy, one may ask the question whether the scope of the Ecodesign Directive should not be enlarged. When the Ecodesign Directive was originally drafted in 2004/2005, it only aimed at energy efficiency. Nowadays, resource and raw materials efficiency has also become an important topic of EU policy. I do not see any arguments which should plead against principally enlarging the focus of the Ecodesign Directive to make it 'fit for purpose' to serve broader environmental goals, including the promotion of the circular economy.

To enlarge the scope of the application of the Ecodesign Directive and to let it serve circular economy purposes, the Commission wants to explore "the possibility of establishing more product-specific and/or horizontal requirements in areas such as durability (e.g. minimum life-time of products or critical components), reparability (e.g. availability of spare parts and repair manuals, design for repair), upgradeability, design for disassembly (e.g. easy removal of certain components), information (e.g. marking of plastic parts) and ease of reuse and recycling (e.g. avoiding incompatible plastics), greenhouse gas and other emissions, and to further establish the scientific basis for developing corresponding criteria that meet the requirements of the Ecodesign Directive".[65] Furthermore, the Commission has asked European standardisation organisations to develop generic standards on the durability, reusability and recyclability of certain products.[66] This seems to be an important step in the right

65 European Commission, Ecodesign Working Plan, COM(2016) 773 final, p. 9.
66 Report from the Commission on the implementation of the Circular Economy Action Plan, 26 January 2017, COM(2017) 33 final, p. 5 f.

direction. These standards should preferably lead to holistic criteria on the environmental effects, amongst which energy efficiency and circularity of certain (groups of) products. However, nothing in the EU Action Plan, the working programme and the first annual report on the implementation is said about the level of standard setting. From a viewpoint of fostering innovations however, mainly the level of the targets is decisive. If the future criteria on resource efficiency are built on what the producers qualify as the current state of the art or on what can be realised quite easily, innovations will not be stimulated. If the transition to a circular economy has to be realised within reasonable time and innovations should be fostered substantially, an ambitious level of standards should be chosen.

6.3 CIRCULAR BUILDING MATERIALS

Construction and demolition are amongst the biggest sources of waste within Europe. They account for approximately 25% – 30% of all waste generated in the EU. The construction and use of buildings in the EU account for about half of all our extracted materials and energy consumption and about a third of our water consumption.[67] In the Netherlands, construction and demolition waste (CDW) is even higher at 40%. Construction activities in the Netherlands count for ca. 50% of all use of materials, 30% of the use of water and 35% of the CO_2-emissions.[68] Therefore, enhancing the circularity in the building sector can really make a difference and should be an important policy aim.

67 European Commission, Communication on Resource Efficiency Opportunities in the Building Sector, COM(2014) 445 final, p. 2.

68 Rijksbreed programma Circulaire Economie, p. 60.

Article 11 of the Waste Framework Directive (2008/98/EC, WFD) addresses CDW. Article 11 (2) WFD stipulates that "Member States shall take the necessary measures designed to achieve that by 2020 a minimum of 70% (by weight) of non-hazardous construction and demolition waste ... shall be prepared for reuse, recycled or undergo other material recovery" (including backfilling operations using waste to substitute other materials). Technology for the separation and recovery of construction and demolition waste is well established, readily accessible and in general inexpensive. Despite its potential, the level of recycling and material recovery of CDW varies greatly (between less than 10% to over 90%) across the Union.[69] According to the Dutch government this is even 95% in the Netherlands.[70] Therefore, one could claim that a circular economy is already realised, at least in the Netherlands and that applying the approach of some frontrunner member states like Germany, the UK or the Netherlands EU-wide, is sufficient. That, however, is not true. The area of CDW demonstrates that focussing only on the percentages of reuse of materials is not sufficient. CDW can be subdivided in two categories. In the groundworks and road-construction sector, almost all materials are reused for similar purposes, therefore at the same or at least comparable level of quality. The materials which were used to construct a road can be reused for the construction of roads. This, however, is different in the second sector, the construction of buildings-sector. Materials from old buildings are usually not used again for the construction of new buildings, but often as filling materials in groundworks and the construction of roads, thus for a lower purpose (downgrading). In the construction of buildings only a very low per-

69 European Commission, Closing the Loop – an EU action plan for the Circular Economy, COM(2015), 614 final, p. 16.

70 Rijksbreed programma Circulaire Economie, p. 60.

centage of secondary materials is applied.[71] The challenge for the years to come is, at least in the frontrunner member states, to extent this high quality reuse of CDW. This can lead to much higher savings of raw materials, water, energy and CO_2. According to the programme of the Dutch government on the circular economy, ground- and roadworks will need less filling materials in the future.[72] Therefore, the reuse of CDW materials in the construction of buildings will not only lead to more savings of materials, water and energy, but will also prevent a surplus of CDW secondary materials, which then would become a threat to the environment. At the same time, the saturation of the market for filling materials in ground- and roadworks brings about economically favourable conditions for enhancing the reuse of these materials in the construction of buildings sector. The question to be discussed is whether the existing legal framework is sufficient to support or even constrain a higher percentage of the use of secondary materials in the construction of the buildings sector.

However even more than enhancing the amount of secondary materials used in the construction of the buildings sector is desirable and possible. Most of the buildings currently standing in the EU and currently built will still be used in 2050. The focus should change from the amount of materials (in weight) which are recycled and reused and the level of that recycling and reuse to the very first phase of the cycle: the design of the construction of buildings. Resource use is determined largely by design deci-

71 Technopolis Group, Regulatory Barriers for the Circular Economy, report 30 June, Amsterdam 2016, p. 44.
72 Rijksbreed programma Circulaire Economie, p. 61.

sions and choices over construction materials.[73] If we, even after 40 years of use,

- know which materials were used in a building,
- if these materials can be disassembled and separated easily
- are suitable for high quality reuse,

the gains of circular solutions can be realised easily and cheap. Circular buildings are designed in such a way that all materials are suitable for high quality reuse or recycling. Ensuring that the above mentioned three criteria are observed in all buildings which are constructed or substantially renovated now, is an investment in the future, which will pay off within 10, 20 or 40 years. As these positive effects on our economy and environment, and by implication on profit and planet too, are long-term effects and as it is necessary to observe the above mentioned criteria in as many new constructed or renovated buildings as possible, there is a need to regulate these requirements. Another argument for regulation is that the costs of environmental damage caused by lavishing raw materials is neither internalised in the landfill fees, nor in the costs of most virgin materials.[74] Therefore, market incentives to enhance circular use of raw materials are absent or not sufficient.

On EU-level, not much action seems to be planned in this regard. A first measure is, as said, the target for 2020 of 70% recycling (including backfilling) for all CDW which is obligatory already now according to Article 11 (2) sub (b) Waste

73 European Commission, Communication on Resource Efficiency Opportunities in the Building Sector, COM(2014) 445 final, p. 2.

74 European Commission, Communication on Resource Efficiency Opportunities in the Building Sector, COM(2014) 445 final, p. 8.

Framework Directive.[75] The action plan does not increase this target. A positive effect of increasing the amount of CDW which is recycled, from a now EU wide 46% to 70% and enforcing such a rate throughout the EU will be that more secondary materials will come available. For countries like Germany, Belgium and the Netherlands,[76] however, these targets are, at best, irrelevant as recycling rates are already much higher. More important, these rates concentrate on the wrong parameters. They lead to a concentration on the efforts to the recycling of heavy materials (concrete, brick, etc.), neglecting the question which materials are the most valuable from a circular economy point of view.

According to the EU action plan, "the commission will develop targeted guidelines for the use of CDW. It will help to spread best practices by developing voluntary recycling protocols based on the highest common standards for each waste stream".[77] All that may be a first, positive step. However, the high potential of the building sector for the reduction of the use of (raw) materials, energy, water and emissions and the long lifetime of buildings plead for further and stronger action. Different from what the EU 2020 package did in 2007 with regards to energy targets for 2020, the action plan on the circular economy does not set comparable targets for the resource efficiency or circularity of constructions and buildings. This is an omission. Mid- and long-term targets on the circularity of construction works and buildings are needed as a motor for national policies, industries and the whole society. There is no EU directive on the 'circu-

75 European Commission, Closing the Loop – an EU action plan for the Circular Economy, COM(2015), 614 final, p. 19.
76 The same is true for the UK, but EU regulation will obviously become less relevant there.
77 European Commission, Closing the Loop – an EU action plan for the Circular Economy, COM(2015), 614 final, p. 16 and 17.

larity performance' or an overall environmental performance of buildings yet. Since 2002, there exists however a directive on the energy performance of buildings (directive 2010/31/EU, which is an amended recast of directive 2002/91/EC). Energy performance has been in the focus of EU policy and the EU lawmaker to enable the reduction of the energy dependence of the EU and to meet the CO_2 reduction targets. This focus should be broadened and should also cover the circularity of buildings.

A prerequisite for setting such targets is the definition of common and unified indicators of environmental performance, amongst which indicators for circularity performance. The Commission wants to develop such indicators to assess the environmental performance throughout the lifecycle of a building. The EU-wide indicators on the environmental performance of buildings can then be prescribed in a similar way as the energy performance requirements now in Articles 4 ff of the energy performance of buildings directive. Using and broadening this existing legal framework is not only quicker and more efficient than proposing a new directive or regulation. It also makes sense in terms of content. Energy-efficiency and raw material efficiency are closely related and intertwined issues. For example, some solutions to improve the energy efficiency of a building in the in-use phase could later make recycling more difficult and expensive which also may have negative effects on the energy consumption of the building materials. If the circularity of the design is not taken into account when fostering the energy efficiency of a building, in sum this may have adverse effects. Article 5 Energy Efficiency Directive requires that 3% of the buildings owned and occupied by central governments have to be renovated each year to realise at least minimum energy performance requirements. According to Article 4 of the same directive, member states have to develop a long-term renovation strategy for their entire building stock. However, buildings are only renovated every 30 or 40 years. The requirement of the Energy Efficiency Directive to renovate buildings should also be used to realise circular building principles. Silo thinking and silo regulating does not make much sense. EU policy on buildings requires a holistic view. All environmental effects of buildings should be taken into account. Therefore, the existing Energy Efficiency Directive and the Energy Performance of Buildings Directive should both be broadened and should take all environmental effects of buildings into account.[78] A different, perhaps even more easy and efficient, strategy would be to only broaden the Energy Performance of Buildings Directive and let it become an Environmental Performance of Buildings Directive. By incorporating a cross reference in the Environmental Performance of Buildings Directive to (at least) Articles 4 and 5 Energy Efficiency Directive, it can be assured that the renovations which have to be undertaken on the basis of the latter directive have to meet the holistic criteria of the Environmental Performance of Buildings Directive and will therefore also support circular building principles.

Recently, more exactly since 2013, such holistic criteria and indicators have been prescribed in Dutch building law. These indicators have been developed within a "Green deal calculation of environmental performance of buildings". The basis for such indicators are, amongst others, the international BREEAM

78 The same plea is brought forward by P. Mul, S. Roos and J.B. Jutte, Opportunities and barriers for circular procurement in the built environment, Paper, Royal Haskoning, July 2016, p. 11; available on http://www.globe-eu.org/wp-content/uploads/Globe-BEE-Paper_circular-procurement-built-environment.pdf, lastly reviewed 5 March 2017.

certificates, a private certification initiative. The Dutch Green Building Council participates in this international sustainability assessment method. In the past years, a method was developed and tested to calculate the total environmental performance of buildings on the basis of Lifecycle Analyses (LCAs). Since 2013, Article 5.9 of the Building Regulation (Bouwbesluit) requires to submit a calculation of the environmental performance of all new houses and office buildings larger than 100 m^2 on the basis of certain methods.[79] Until now, the fact that the environmental performance of such buildings is calculated and taken into account is sufficient. However, after five years of gathering experience with the calculation of the environmental performance of buildings, the Dutch government wants to introduce a minimum requirement for the two categories of buildings mentioned in Article 5.9 Building Regulation from January 2018 onwards. This is a logical and consistent development on the way to a more circular and environmentally sound building practice. It should be followed by similar requirements for other categories of buildings. However, the proposed criterion of 1 euro/m^2 [80] does not seem to be ambitious at all. An Agency of the Dutch government, the Rijksdienst voor Ondernemend Nederland (RVO), proposes criteria between 0,22€ and 0,65€ for homes and 0,70€ and 0,90€ for offices.[81] What is noticeable is, that the Dutch government does not even seem to want to set ambitious targets

79 The so called 'Bepalingsmethode milieuprestatie van gebouwen en GWW-werken'.

80 What this means, can be deducted from the calculation tool "Bepaling van de milieuprestaties van gebouwen en gww-werken; https://www.rijksoverheid.nl/documenten/brochures/2015/02/05/bepaling-van-de-milieuprestaties-van-gebouwen-en-gww-werken-mpg; lastly reviewed 4 March 2017.

81 RVO, Milieu Prestatie Gebouwen, Praktijkwaarden MPG-berekeningen, http://www.rvo.nl/onderwerpen/duurzaam-ondernemen/gebouwen/wetten-en-regels-gebouwen/milieuprestatie-gebouwen, lastly reviewed 5 March 2017.

and requirements. In conformity with its recent general policy in the environmental area, the government wants to limit the ambition of the national government and leave it to the municipalities to conclude more far reaching requirements. In order to do so, the new Buildings and the Living Environment Order (Besluit bouwwerken leefomgeving (Bbl)), an order on the basis of the new Environment and Planning Act (Omgevingswet, Ow) shall empower the municipalities to set higher standards in their Physical Environment Plan (omgevingsplan). I doubt whether this extreme and somewhat doctrinal practice of decentralisation makes much sense.

Efficient circular building will not be realised and innovative solutions will not be fostered by local setting of standards and requirements, but need to make use of the economies of scale. That urges for ambitious and clear standard setting at least on national, even better on European level.[82] There is a risk that the indicators which at the moment are developed in several member states will differ, leading to an unnecessarily complex business environment.[83] The developments in the private sector are similar. Besides the already mentioned BREEAM, there are some other private certification schemes. However, uptake of certification is hampered by the uncertainty as to whether an assessment scheme will be required by the final client and if so, according to which specific scheme. There is no established comparability between the different schemes which also adds to

82 P. Mul, S. Roos and J.B. Jutte, Opportunities and barriers for circular procurement in the built environment, Paper, Royal Haskoning, July 2016, p. 6; available on http://www.globe-eu.org/wp-content/uploads/Globe-BEE-Paper_circular-procurement-built-environment.pdf, lastly reviewed 5 March 2017.

83 European Commission, Communication on Resource Efficiency Opportunities in the Building Sector, COM(2014) 445 final, p. 4.

the uncertainty and complexity for businesses[84] and hinders the application of economies of scale. I cannot judge whether the Dutch standards and calculation schemes should be upgraded to EU level or whether other schemes and standards are more adequate. However, it seems clear to me that harmonising such criteria and schemes on EU level and developing a common framework for lifecycle analyses for environmental performance of buildings should be a priority for the EU. These standards may be based on Article 3 Construction Products Regulation (Regulation 305/2011/EU). Annex I, sub 7 Construction Products Regulation already mentions the following as 'basic requirement for construction works': "construction works must be designed, built and demolished in such a way that the use of natural resources is sustainable and in particular ensure the following:

(a) reuse or recyclability of the construction works, their materials and parts after demolition;
(b) durability of the construction works;
(c) use of environmentally compatible raw and secondary materials in the construction works."

The regulation also mentions other environmental issues as basic requirements, like emissions and energy efficiency. Therefore, the legal basis to prescribe environmental standards of construction works and their separate parts already seems to be present. However, the criteria mentioned in Annex I, sub 7 Construction Products Regulation are not yet made concrete and therefore not yet applied in practice. The investment in common and clear standards for lifecycle analyses for environmental performance of buildings and binding targets, including a 'building passport'

84 European Commission, Communication on Resource Efficiency Opportunities in the Building Sector, COM(2014) 445 final, p. 4.

could change that. This seems to be an essential prerequisite to encourage the construction sector to invest in circular building materials and building solutions.[85] In its communication on Resource Efficiency Opportunities in the Building Sector from 2014, the Commission announced to develop such a common framework with core indicators and their underlying methods. However, the Commission does not aim at integrating all aspects of environmental performance, but wants to limit the framework to "the indicators that after the consultation with stakeholders have been identified as the ones with the highest environmental impact in the EU". As more comprehensive and holistic sets of indicators are already available in practice, this self-restraint is regrettable. Holistic environmental performance standards should not only support voluntary action, but should become obligatory for all new buildings and substantial renovations throughout the EU. As we have seen above, this is necessary to foster innovations, to facilitate and simplify circular public procurement and to utilise economies of scale.

6.4 STIMULATING GREEN PUBLIC PROCUREMENT

Public procurement accounts for a large proportion of European consumption (nearly 20% of EU GDP).[86] In financial terms, this is more than 2.000 billion euros. Therefore, public procurement can play an important role as an engine on the way of the transition to a circular economy. In this regard, the EU and the EU

85 See also P. Mul, S. Roos and J.B. Jutte, Opportunities and barriers for circular procurement in the built environment, Paper, Royal Haskoning, July 2016, p. 7; available on http://www.globe-eu.org/wp-content/uploads/Globe-BEE-Paper_circular-procurement-built-environment.pdf, lastly reviewed 5 March 2017.

86 European Commission, Closing the Loop – an EU action plan for the Circular Economy, COM(2015), 614 final, p. 8.

Commission have a twofold role. First, the Commission wants to lead by example when placing orders. It aims at stressing efficient use of resources in its own public procurement procedures. Second, and more important, it is crucial that European public procurement law enables or even forces public authorities in the member states to realise 'circular procurement'.[87] The relevant criteria are to be found in directives 2014/23/EU, 2014/24/EU and 2014/25/EU. I will only deal with directive 2014/24/EU on public procurement, which is perceived as the most central piece of law of the European public procurement law.[88] One of the main goals of the recent amendment of the directives was to facilitate and stimulate green public procurement (GPP). GPP is defined by the European Commission as "a process whereby public authorities seek to procure goods, services and works with a reduced environmental impact throughout their lifecycle when compared to goods, services and works with the same primary function that would otherwise be procured".[89]

A basic requirement of procurement law is that contracting authorities shall base the award of public contracts on the most economically advantageous tender (Article 67 (1) Public Procurement Directive). Therefore, the question which kind of costs may or must be calculated is a crucial one. According to Article 67 (2) Public Procurement Directive, the most economically advantageous tender shall be identified on the basis of the price or cost, using a cost-effectiveness approach, such as lifecycle costing. In assessing the prices or costs, qualitative, environmental and

87 More specifically detailed: S. Schoenmaekers, Aanbesteding en duurzaamheid, een natuurlijke symbiose, M en R 2016/2.

88 Directive 2014/25/EU concern purchasing in the water, energy, transport and postal sectors and directive 2014/23/EU concern concession contracts.

89 European Commission, Public Procurement for a better environment, COM(2008) 400.

social aspects, linked to the subject-matter of the public contract in question, may be taken into account. This crucial provision is elaborated further in Article 68 Public Procurement Directive, which clarifies amongst others, that end of life costs, such as collection and recycling costs (Article 68 (1) (a) (iii)) and costs imputed to environmental externalities linked to the product, service or works during its lifecycle (Article 68 (1) (b)) belong to the 'lifecycle costing'. That is an extensive range. According to the preamble lifecycle costing also comprises costs "such as pollution caused by extraction of the raw materials used in the product".[90] It is not necessary that the application of all these criteria financially favours the public authority as the directive entails that public authorities may take non-economic motives and considerations into account.[91] On the basis of this amendment and enlargement of the scope of the public procurement rules, it is now possible to take all environmental costs of products or services into account when awarding a contract, including (raw) material efficiency and use of secondary material. That is an enormous step forward. However, a prerequisite is that the environmental effects, like circularity criteria, can be expressed in objective monetary terms.

Innovation can be fostered if awarding criteria are drafted as functional or performance criteria and not as technical standards. Tenderers can comply with functional criteria in very different ways. If functional and performance criteria are used instead of precise technical standards, artificially narrowing down competition is avoided and innovation is favoured as much as possible. It is then possible to award those tenders

90 Consideration 96 of Directive 2014/24/EU.

91 This was already decided in ECJ 17 September 2002, C-513/99 (Concordia Bus Finland).

that are the most sustainable ones.[92] Prescribing specific technical requirements, like the use of certain production methods, filters or other techniques will, at least in a long-term, hamper innovation. The same may be true for prescribing certain certificates. The new directive facilitates the use of such certificates in the awarding criteria, partly in reaction to the Dutch coffee vending machine-judgment of the Court of Justice.[93] Although prescribing certificates may favour environmental aspects in the decision making, it may not foster innovations in environmental optimisation. Whether it does or not depends on the criteria used in the certification audit. If these criteria comprise detailed technical standards, innovation is rather hampered than supported. If these criteria leave ample room to the tenderers in how to comply, innovation may be encouraged.

Finally, attention should be drawn to the newly introduced Article 31, which makes it possible to set up 'innovation partnerships'. Such an innovation partnership is a long-term coalition between the public authority and one or more enterprises. According to Article 31 Public Procurement Directive, "in the procurement documents, the contracting authority shall identify the need for an innovative product, service or works that cannot be met by purchasing products, services or works already available on the market". In such cases the procurement could be characterised as a combination of the mutual creation of a new (type of) product, work or service and the purchasing of this new product, work or service by the authority. Establishing such partnerships should simplify the creation of new, innovative products or services. When selecting the possible tender-

92 See also preamble 74 of directive 2014/24/EU.
93 CJEU 10 May 2012, C-368/10 (Cie. vs. Nederland).

ers for such an innovation partnership, the authority should, according to Article 31 (6), pay specific attention to the research and development potential of the candidates and their ability to develop new solutions. It could happen that this new provision will become important for Dutch and international green deals, especially the Dutch green deal on circular procurement.[94] This green deal aims at practically facilitating the transition to circular procurement and has gathered quite some experience with lots of pilot projects. Since May 2016 there is also an European innovation deal. However, this EU pilot "innovation deals for a circular economy" seems to be comparable with the Dutch 'Ruimte voor Regels steunpunt.' In essence it safeguards that enterprises can report to the Commission if existing EU law is hampering innovative solutions fostering the circular economy. Until June 2016, 32 issues have been reported to the Commission. The Commission has announced to investigate two of these cases further.[95]

However, until now, the role of the Commission in this area has been a limited one. In the end, it is above all the member states that have to procure their contracts and, when doing so, *may* take into account criteria that foster a circular economy. Directive 2014/24/EU does not require member states to procure circular and sustainable. In her action plan, the Commission is very clear about this: the Commission shall develop criteria for circular procurement which then can be "used by public authorities on a voluntary basis".[96] Furthermore, the Commission wants

94 See http://mvonederland.nl/green-deal-circulair-inkopen.

95 See the Conclusions of the Council on the action plan Circular Economy of 21 June 2016, 10518, p. 5. See also the report of the Commission on the implementation of the Circular Economy Action Plan, of 26 January 2017, COM(2017) 33 final, p. 4 ff.

96 EU-action plan on a circular economy, COM(2015) 0614 final, p. 7 f.

to facilitate a broader application of GPP, for example through targeted training schemes, and wants to lead by example with regards to her own procurements. However, if EU politicians (and thus member states) would want to, the EU legislator could do much more and could prescribe (a certain amount of) GPP. This idea is rejected in the preamble of the directive, at least with regards to general mandatory requirements. This would not be adequate because of "the important differences between individual sectors and markets".[97] It is absolutely right that a detailed, quantified obligation of GPP does not seem to make much sense. However, I do not agree with the restraint in general. It would be a valuable signal and message if the Public Procurement Directive would prescribe that member states' authorities are obliged to always take into account environmental aspects, including energy efficiency and efficient use of (raw) materials in their procurements. However, specific, quantified targets for certain groups of products, works and services would be even more effective. There are already examples for such a thing as is demonstrated by the directive 2009/33/EU on the promotion of clean and energy efficient road transport vehicles. This directive obliges the authorities of the member states to consider energy efficiency and environmental performances in their procurement criteria. The directive also harmonises how these criteria should be evaluated and weighed. Currently, the scope of the directive is limited to mainly energy efficiency and emissions, although member state authority "may also consider other environmental impacts".[98] Legally, there is nothing to be barred to enlarge the scope of this directive and to, for example, prescribe the amount of secondary materials used in the production of

97 Preamble 95 of Directive 2014/24/EU.

98 Article 5 (2) Directive 2009/33/EC.

cars, purchased by public authorities. This could have a tremendous effect on the transparency of the circularity of these products and on the broad market introduction and dissemination of more circular cars. The same holds true for other groups of products, for example buildings[99] or computers and other office appliances.

We can conclude that the EU law, after its revision in 2014, now offers broad options for GPP, However, EU law and the policy of the Commission are optional and aim at voluntary actions of the member states' authorities. A very important way to encourage and facilitate GPP are the EU Green Public Procurement Criteria, published by the Commission with regards to quite some groups of products. These documents prescribe in detail which criteria can be chosen to make procurements greener. Comparing older with more recent documents, it becomes clear that criteria fostering the circular economy become more prominent recently.[100] These documents however prove that it would, without further ado, be technically possible to prescribe GPP for many sectors and groups of products, if the political willingness were there.

---

99 Directive 2010/31/EU on the energy performance of buildings has a much more narrow scope.

100 See for example EU GPP Criteria for Office Building Design, Construction and Management, SWD(2016) 180 (final); all documents can be found at http://ec.europa.eu/environment/gpp/eu_gpp_criteria_en.htm, lastly reviewed 27 February 2017.

7. SUMMARY AND CONCLUDING REMARKS

THE CIRCULAR ECONOMY AS A PATHWAY TO SUSTAINABILITY

If we would continue our way of life and the emerging countries would adapt to our current standards, we would need nine to fifteen earths to provide the resources needed. There is no choice to opt for or against a dramatic reduction of our use of primary resources. We only have one earth and have to radically change our way of producing and consuming to make it sustainable.[101] One of the pathways to sustainability is the circular economy. What we can choose is whether we want to be a frontrunner on this pathway, which probably will offer huge economical possibilities and long-term gains, or whether we only want to be a follower, which may cost less investments in the short term. To enhance the efficiency of political strategies on a sustainable use of resources, concrete mid- and long-term targets seem to be urgently needed on EU and national level. Governments should quickly agree on a common terminology and methodology to measure the use of primary resources and the effectiveness of their reduction policies.

NUMEROUS AND DIVERSE LEGAL QUESTIONS

Fostering the circular economy touches upon and creates a great variety of legal questions in many different areas of law which have to be addressed and answered in an interdisciplinary

101 See also the arguments of the Dutch Social and Economic Council (SER), Werken aan een circulaire economie: geen tijd te verliezen, The Hague 2016, p. 31 ff.

nexus. Utrecht University should be an important player in this field of research.

THE ENVIRONMENT AND PLANNING ACT (OMGEVINGSWET) IS NOT CIRCULAR

In the preparatory documents for the new Dutch Environment and Planning Act (Omgevingswet), the term 'circular economy' is not mentioned. In the Dutch policy strategy on the circular economy (Rijksbreed programma circulaire economie) the focus on the legal aspects is wrongfully limited to the elimination of legal rules that may hinder innovations. It seems fair to say that focusing only on the removal of the present regulatory obstacles that entrepreneurs face today when starting a new circular business, however useful that is, will not be sufficient to make a transition to a circular economy. To realise the circular economy lots of legal frameworks and rules will have to be reconsidered, amended and some completely newly framed. Fostering innovations urges the use of the law for setting ambitious and enforceable requirements and targets. To do so, EU and national legal measures will have to be taken. It is a pity that it has not been the focus of the lawmaker to ensure that the Environment and Planning Act optimally supports the fundamental transitions to sustainability, for instance by focusing on decarbonisation and circularity. The Dutch government should invest in developing the legal infrastructure which is necessary for these pathways to sustainability.

NECESSARY AMENDMENTS OF THE WASTE FRAMEWORK DIRECTIVE

Considerations to limit the scope of waste law should not only focus on the need to manage environmental risks of materials and products, but should also address the question whether the highest possible level of the (re)use of materials or goods will be assured if waste law is abandoned.

The following suggestions are made to improve the EU Waste Framework Directive in order to foster the circular economy. Article 5 of this directive should be broadened and should apply to all kind of materials and goods, not only to so-called 'by-products'. The European Commission should be empowered to exclude, on a case-by-case basis, certain products and materials from the waste regime if (a) further use is certain, (b) lawful and (c) contributes to a high level of efficient use of primary materials. Such a possibility to exclude the application of waste law would make it possible to foster circular solutions which may now be hindered by the applicability of waste law if it is proven that the continued (re)use will not contravene waste hierarchy strategies and other environmental and resource efficiency requirements and goals.

EU AND NATIONAL LEGAL REGIME ON INDUSTRIAL PRODUCTION – NO INCENTIVES FOR INNOVATIONS

European Commission tries to enhance resource efficiency in production processes mainly by including this aspect in the BREF documents. This will not foster innovations. If we want to exploit EU-regulation on industrial production to foster innovations for the circular economy, national governments must take the lead and prescribe circular economy norms in general rules on permit conditions which go beyond BAT and beyond what is required by European law. In this area, because of the structure of EU the relevant EU law, 'goldplating' (nationale koppen) is needed and should not be discredited.

LEGAL INSTRUMENTS TO FOSTER CIRCULAR PRODUCTS AND CIRCULAR BUILDINGS

The Ecodesign Directive should be used more intensively to promote circular products and especially to encourage innovation in this area. To make it 'fit for purpose' to optimally serve the aim of the reduction of primary materials use, the scope of the Ecodesign Directive should be enlarged. Holistic criteria on the environmental effects, amongst which energy efficiency and circularity, of certain (groups of) products should be developed.

Investing in circular buildings now, will pay off within 10, 20 or 40 years. Therefore, market incentives to enhance circular use of raw materials in buildings are absent or too low. Binding EU mid and long-term targets on the circularity of buildings are needed as a motor for national policies and industries. These targets can be based on the directive on the energy performance of buildings (directive 2010/31/EU) which should become an Environmental Performance of Buildings Directive. Silo thinking and silo regulating does not make much sense. EU policy and law on buildings require a holistic view which takes into account all environmental effects of buildings. By adding a cross reference to Articles 4 and 5 Energy Efficiency Directive, the requirement to renovate buildings within a certain time can also be used to realise circular building principles.

This requires the development of holistic methods to calculate the environmental performance of buildings on EU level. Developing a common framework for lifecycle analyses for environmental performance of buildings should be a priority for the EU. In the Netherlands, such criteria were developed and have to be applied on the basis of Article 5.9 of the Dutch Building Order. This may serve as an example, but also other sets of standards may be chosen. This seems to be an essential prerequisite to encourage the construction sector to invest in circular building materials and building solutions. However, innovation will only be stimulated if holistic requirements on the environmental performance are set at an ambitious level. The recently proposed requirement based on Article 5.9 of the Dutch Building order is not such an ambitious criterion and does not encourage innovation. To only empower the municipalities to set higher standards in their Physical Environment Plan (omgevingsplan) is not a good choice.

CIRCULAR PUBLIC PROCUREMENT LAW

Public procurement accounts for a large proportion of European consumption (nearly 20% of EU GDP). It therefore can play an important role as an engine on the way of the transition to a circular economy. The recent revision of the EU public procurement directives means an enormous step forward for the possibilities of green public procurement. To foster innovations, circular awarding criteria should always be drafted as functional or performance criteria and not as technical standards. It would be a valuable signal if the Public Procurement Directive would prescribe that member states authorities are obliged to always take into account environmental aspects, including energy efficiency and efficient use of (raw) materials in their procurements. Besides that, specific, quantified targets for certain groups of products, works and services would be effective to foster the circular economy. For example, on the basis of Directive 2009/33/EU the amount of secondary materials used in the production of cars, purchased by public authorities, could be prescribed. This could have a tremendous effect on the transparency of the circularity of these products and on the broad market introduction and dissemination of more circular cars.

8. WORDS OF THANKS

The habit to complete an inaugural address with some words of thanks is not without reason. I want to again emphasize something I already said in my third inaugural address in 2008. To be permitted and to be able to accept an appointment as professor by delivering an inaugural address is in the first place not something the orator has deserved because of his own merits. At least in my case I owe this chance to many people.

Ik dank de rector, het college van bestuur en de benoemingscommissie voor het, wederom, in mij gestelde vertrouwen.

Geachte decaan, geacht faculteitsbestuur,

u hebt er nog een schepje bovenop gedaan door mij na korte tijd al als facultair gezant op pad te sturen om als een van de "makers" een kwartier te bouwen voor het universitair strategisch programma sustainability. Ik hoop dat ik een steentje aan het maken van dit kwartier heb bijgedragen en ook in de toekomst nog kan zorgen voor bijvoorbeeld wat ramen die heldere zichtlijnen mogelijk maken.

Beste Rob,

toen jij tijdens een terugreis van een gezamenlijke workshop in Brussel mij wat indringender vroeg hoe het gaat in Maastricht en wat mijn toekomstplannen zijn kon ik niet vermoeden dat daar wellicht nog wat anders dan pure nieuwsgierigheid en belangstelling van een zeer bijzondere oud-collega achter zat. Ik dank je voor de bijzondere collegialiteit en vriendschap waarmee wij nu, bijna dertig jaar, samen optrekken, soms intensiever en soms minder intensief. Ik verheug mij niet alleen op het succesvol afsluiten van ons gezamenlijk Ius Commune casebook project, maar op alle mogelijke vormen van samenwerking die er in de pakweg komende 10 jaar nog zullen ontstaan.

Beste Marleen,

hoewel jij niet in de benoemingscommissie zat, zal ook jij, jouw kennende, aardig wat in de melk gebrokkeld hebben. Het is iets bijzonders als een promovendus die men ooit heeft begeleid een paar jaar later jouw baas wordt. Zo is het bij ons gegaan en dat werkt heel goed. Minstens zo belangrijk: het is volledig terecht. Ik bewonder hoe jij met enorme werkkracht, visie en enthousiasme het Centre for Water, Oceans and Sustainability Law hebt opgebouwd en wat jij ervan hebt gemaakt. De uitstekende kwaliteit is onlangs in de onderzoeksvisitatie op indrukwekkende wijze bevestigd. Ik hoop dat wij deze groei en bloei in het komende decennium op even inspirerende wijze kunnen voortzetten.

Beste Ton en Remco,

jullie hebben mij warm en met open deuren en harten onthaald op ASP 200. Dat ervaar ik als grote steun bij het werk. Veel dank daarvoor!

Dear members of UCWOSL,

the only fault of UCWOSL is its acronym. You all are a vivid and enormously inspiring research group. Every day I relish to be part of this flourishing and stimulating environment.

Beste leden van de Afdeling SBR,

het is een genoegen om weer 'terug' te zijn, maar het is toch te merken dat de Afdeling is doorontwikkeld en met veel elan nieuwe ideeën uittest om onderwijs en onderzoek op een nog hoger niveau te brengen. Ik verheug mij op de samenwerking met velen van jullie.

Beste Christine,

je was een niet te missen steun bij de voorbereiding van al dit (en hetgeen vanavond nog komt)! Dank hiervoor en in het bijzonder voor het geduld wanneer ik voor de zoveelste keer weer met een aanvulling op de genodigdenlijst kwam.

Dames en heren studenten,

uw kritische bijdragen en vragen zijn essentieel niet alleen voor mijn pogingen om kwalitatief goed onderwijs te geven, maar, en dat zult u wellicht minder vermoeden, ook voor mijn onderzoek. Het samen met Frank Groothuijse verzorgen van de mastervakken omgevingsrecht was een genot. Ik was zeer onder de indruk van wat jullie aan de eind van het traject allemaal konden. Blijf kritisch en gedreven.

Liebe Trude,

ich bin besonders glücklich, dass Du mit gut neunzig Jahren noch so fit bist und heute mit uns sein und feiern kannst. Das ich diesen Weg gehen konnte, liegt zu einem wesentlichen Teil auch an den Eigenschaften und Fähigkeiten, die Du und Hanns mir mitgegeben und vermittelt haben. Dafür von Herzen Dank!

Liebe Coesfelder,

es ist sehr wertvoll und bereichernd, Euch an meiner Seite zu haben. In schwierigeren Zeiten ward ihr für Sarah und mich ein enormer Rückhalt und seid das auch heute noch. Vielen Dank dafür!

Liebe Sarah,

ohne Dich wäre ich wahrscheinlich heute auch Professor – aber lange nicht so ein glücklicher. Es macht viel Spaß, Dich auf Deinem spannenden, und dazu auch noch erfolgreichen Lebensweg zu sehen und ein klein wenig zu begleiten.

Lieve, dear, liebe Anette,

in welcher Sprache auch immer und ob in Maastricht, Berlin oder Südamerika: das Leben mit Dir ist ein Genuss und voller Freude. Ich hätte mir nicht träumen lassen, dass ich mit einem Menschen so glücklich werden könnte. Ich hoffe, dass zusammen mit Dir noch lange Zeit zu bleiben.

Ik heb gezegd.